SAUROPODS
(giant dinosaurs)

STEGOSAURS
(plated dinosaurs)

STEGOSAURS
(plated dinosaurs)

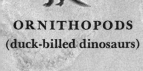

ORNITHOPODS
(duck-billed dinosaurs)

SAUROPODS
(giant dinosaurs)

SAUROPODS
(giant dinosaurs)

THE GIANT
GOLDEN BOOK
OF

DINO

SAURS

and Other Prehistoric Reptiles

by Jane Werner Watson

Illustrated by Rudolph F. Zallinger

A GOLDEN BOOK · NEW YORK
Western Publishing Company, Inc.
Racine, Wisconsin 53404

CONTENTS

Library of Congress Catalog Card Number: 60-14884

GOLDEN®, GOLDEN & DESIGN®, and A GOLDEN BOOK® are trademarks
of Western Publishing Company, Inc.

ISBN 0-307-13764-3

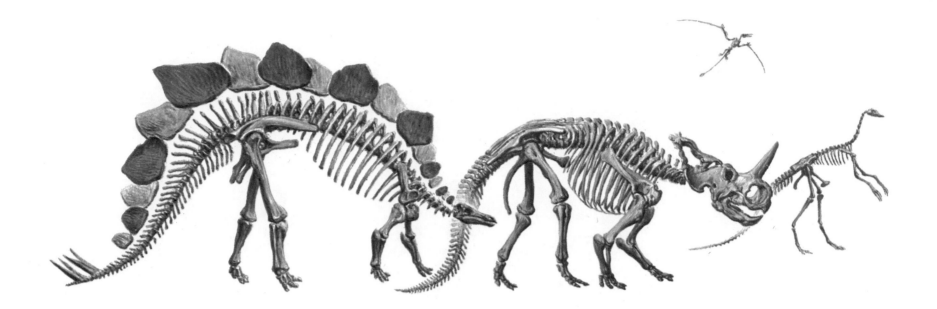

Fishes of the Devonian Period

Lobe-finned fishes of Devonian Period come on land.

BEFORE THE DINOSAURS

THE DINOSAURS lived long, long ago. More than two hundred million years ago the first dinosaurs appeared. About seventy million years ago, the last of them disappeared.

That is a long, long time ago. It is hard for us even to imagine such a long time, but let us try.

Perhaps the line at the bottom of the pages of this book will help us. It is a time line. It runs all the way back to the time of the first dinosaurs. The line starts below on the opposite page with the present, today. All the long years from today back through history fit into the tiny red space below—about six thousand years.

Before man learned to write his story, he had lived for about one million years. Man had spent a long, long time learning to gather food and to build shelters. He had spent a long time learning to live in groups. But on our time line all that time fits into the small orange space below.

Let us look back before the days of human beings. For long ages before man appeared, the chief kinds of animals were mammals. Mammals are the furry kinds of animals we know best today—the dogs and cats, the elephants and bears, the wild beasts large and small. What we call the "Age of Mammals" is shown in yellow on our time line.

Back, back through seventy million years ago goes the Age of Mammals. Back to page 19 on our time line it goes. Way back in those early times most mammals were small. Horses were only about the size of small dogs today.

Before the days when mammals became common, the dinosaurs ruled the earth. The Era or Time of the Dinosaurs is shown in green on our time line.

Turn the pages from 19 on. Turn them one by one. Each block stands for a million years—as much time as mankind has lived on earth. The Time of the Dinosaurs stretches for page after page, through millions and millions of years.

The dinosaurs go back to more than two hundred million years ago. But our story goes back even further than that. On page 41 on our time line the first dinosaurs appear. But still the line goes on.

For the dinosaurs did not come out of nowhere. They developed from earlier animals. The time of these earlier animals is shown in blue on our line. Our book would need many more pages to carry the time line back to the beginning of that age. For that age began when the first animals came out of the sea and started living on shore.

The story of the dinosaurs really begins way back then.

6   AGRIOTHERIUM   7   PROCAMELUS   PLIOHIPPUS   8   9   AMPHICYON   10   11

This is the kind of fish that moved ashore to live on land. Its name is OSTEOLEPIS.

This is what early amphibians looked like when they had changed their fins to weak legs and feet. Its name is DIPLOVERTEBRON.

This is an amphibian after some ages of life on land. His name is ERYOPS. *He has grown larger. He can move about slowly on clumsy legs and is rather fierce. His kind still lays eggs in water.*

HOW THE DINOSAURS CAME TO BE

300 to 250 Million Years Ago

THREE hundred million years ago, all of earth's creatures lived in the seas. But very, very gradually some of them learned to live on land. In some places the fish swam up rivers and bays and learned to live in fresh water. Finally there were fishes in rivers, lakes and ponds.

We do not know just what happened. Perhaps some fishes found themselves in rivers or ponds which dried up during certain seasons of the year. When they tried to swim, they flopped onto the mud.

Some of these ancient fishes were lung fishes. They could breathe air. (There are still lung fishes today which live in Africa, Australia and South America. When their rivers and lakes dry up during hot weather, they can still keep alive because they can breathe air.)

Among these ancient lung fishes were some with very strong fins. In water the fishes could move

This is an early reptile which could lay its eggs on land. It could live all its life on land. Its name is SEYMOURIA.

easily. They simply swayed along. Their tails pushed against the water. They steered with their two pairs of fins. And the water itself held them up.

On land it was harder to move but the lobe-finned lung fishes could drag themselves along with their fins.

Year after year after year, these fishes used their rounded fins like feet. They dragged themselves over the mud with their fins, to the next pond. Slowly, slowly those fins grew and changed. They grew longer and stronger. They were no longer needed for swimming. So they developed into what those creatures did need to live on land. Fins developed into legs and feet.

When plants or animals change or develop to fit the way they live, we call the change evolution.

These animals with lungs and feet were not fish any more. But they were not entirely land animals either. They still laid their eggs in water. And their babies lived in water until they grew up.

THIS KIND of creature we call an amphibian, which means "double life." There are still some amphibians which live today. Toads and frogs are amphibians. They live on land, but they lay their jelly-like eggs in water. There the eggs hatch into tadpoles, and the young tadpoles grow up in ponds.

*This is a tuatara (*SPHENODON*). It is a little changed survivor of the ancestors of lizards and dinosaurs. It is found in only one place in the world—on a small island in New Zealand.*

Well, ages went by. Amphibians developed stronger legs and backbones. They could walk without dragging themselves along the ground. They got along very well as long as there were plenty of swamps and ponds.

But the earth was changing. Many lands were being pushed up high above the seas. Many swamps and ponds dried up. This was hard on the amphibians, since they need water to lay their eggs in.

It was about this time that some amphibians made a great change. They began to lay eggs in hard shells.

These hard egg-shells protected the jelly-like eggs. Inside the shells were water and food for the tiny babies. So these eggs did not have to be laid in ponds. They could be laid on dry ground. And when the young animals came out of the eggs, they did not have to live in the water. They could live on land.

Now these animals no longer had to stay near the water. They could go where they pleased. They did not need water to lay their eggs in. They could live all their lives on land. They were a new kind of animal. We call them reptiles.

There are still some reptiles today. Lizards and snakes, turtles and alligators are reptiles. Alligators and turtles are usually found near the water. But some lizards and snakes live where it is very dry.

When reptiles had developed eggs that could be laid on land, they could live in many places where amphibians could not live. They found many new kinds of food.

This is an early reptile called a cotylosaur. His name is LIMNOSCELIS. *They have been extinct for 200 million years, but they were the ancestors of later reptiles.*

EDAPHOSAURUS

DIMETRODON

Some ate fish. Some ate meat. Some ate plants. And they gradually developed different shapes of bones and teeth, to suit the ways they lived and ate. They developed into creatures of all sizes and many shapes.

Think of food. There have always been animals, on land or in the sea, which ate meat. We call them carnivores, meat-eaters. They are usually rather fierce, for they are hunters. They must kill to live.

Carnivores need long, sharp teeth for snatching and tearing food. They need swift legs for running after it.

There have always been plant-eaters too. We call them herbivores. Plant-eaters are usually meek and mild. Even a small carnivore is often fiercer than a big herbivore.

Plants do not run away. So plant-eaters do not need to be able to move fast to get food. (Though it is helpful to be able to run away from carnivores!) What plant-eaters need most is broad, blunt teeth. These are good for chopping up plant food. And they need large stomachs to digest food slowly.

Some reptiles developed teeth which fitted into deep cups in their jawbones. We call these cups "sockets." This whole group of reptiles, which lived about 200 million years ago, scientists call theco-donts. This name means "teeth-in-sockets."

GORGOSAURUS

Reptile-hip

These "teeth-in-sockets" or thecodonts were mostly small animals, with light bones. Their new teeth were sharp. Their hind legs were strong, and they could raise the front part of their bodies from the ground. They could run swiftly. So they got plenty of food. They were successful animals. As ages passed, some of these "teeth-in-sockets" developed into dinosaurs.

WHAT IS a dinosaur? When scientists began to find the bones of these animals of the past in rocks, they were impressed by their great size. The bones were much like those of some lizards of today. But they were much, much larger. So "terrible lizards" seemed a good name for these unknown animals. The word dinosaur comes from two Greek words, *deinos* and *sauros*. "Terrible lizard" is what these words mean.

None of the dinosaurs were really lizards. Not all were terrifying. Many were not even very large. They did not even all belong to the same order of reptiles.

This is how the two orders of dinosaurs came to be. The split started with those swift, light-boned "teeth-in-socket" reptiles. As they raced about the woodlands after food, they found they could run faster on two legs than on four.

They began to run on their hind legs. They used their front legs for snatching at food. Gradually, through many thousands of years, these front limbs became shorter. Often they had hook-like claws on their feet. For balance, they developed long tails.

To run on their hind legs, the animals had to hold their legs under their bodies, as birds do today, instead of sprawled out to the side, like lizards' legs. This change in leg position caused changes in the muscles of legs and hips and in the hip bones too.

Through ages of walking on hind legs, some of these animals developed "bird-hips." Bird-hips have especially deep sockets for the upper leg bones to fit into. And the backbone is especially strongly attached to the hip bones.

The bird-hips are one great order of dinosaurs. Scientists call them Ornithischia. Others made the change in hip bones in a different way. They make up the other great order of dinosaurs. And scientists call them Saurischia or "reptile-hips."

Later on some members of both groups went back to walking on all fours. But they retained the bird-like or reptile-like hip structure.

So to this day a scientist will look at the hip bones of a dinosaur and classify it as a bird-hip or a reptile-hip.

CAMARASAURUS

*Dinosaurs are divided into two orders—
the Saurischia or "reptile-hips"
and the Ornithischia or "bird-hips."*

CAMPTOSAURUS

Bird-hip

STEGOSAURUS

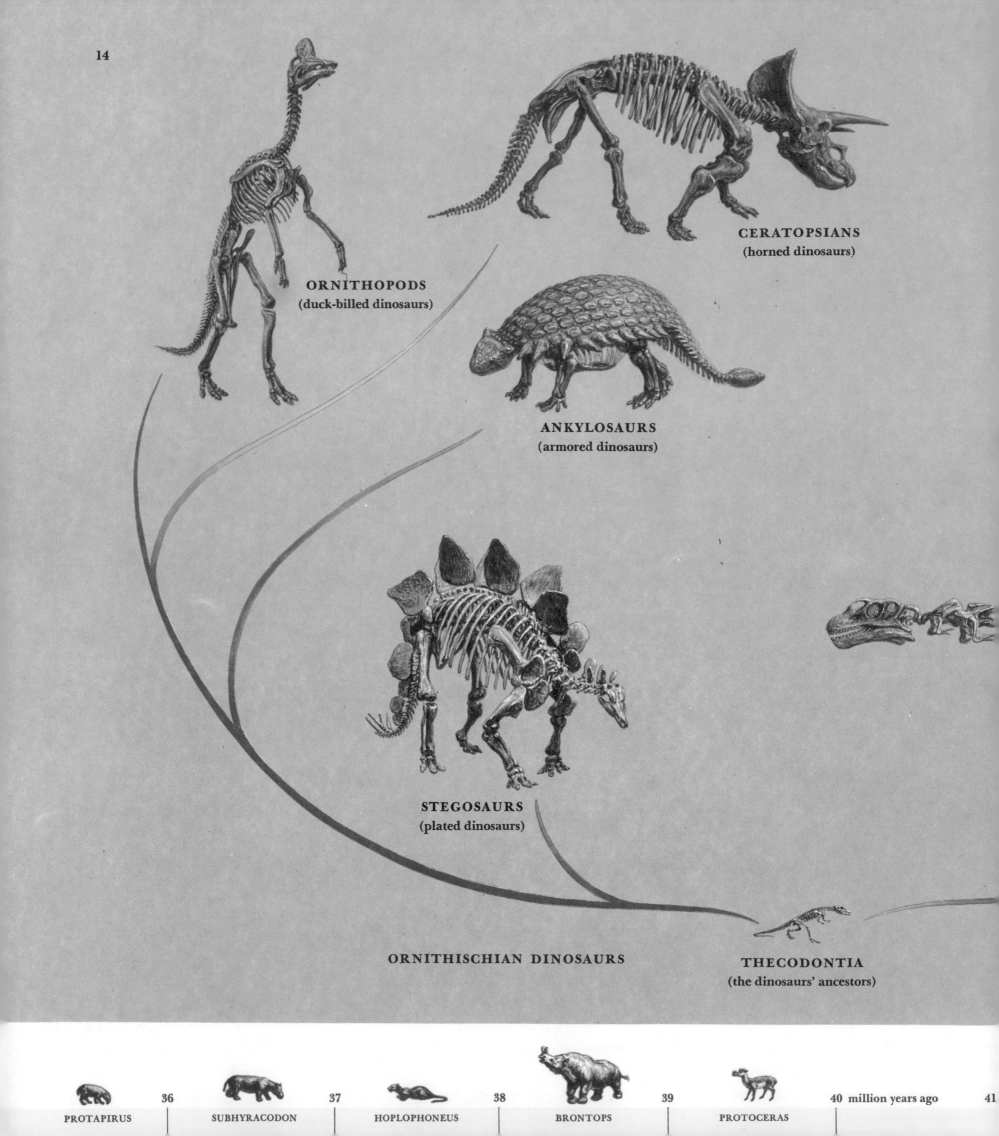

14

ORNITHOPODS
(duck-billed dinosaurs)

CERATOPSIANS
(horned dinosaurs)

ANKYLOSAURS
(armored dinosaurs)

STEGOSAURS
(plated dinosaurs)

ORNITHISCHIAN DINOSAURS

THECODONTIA
(the dinosaurs' ancestors)

PROTAPIRUS 36 SUBHYRACODON 37 HOPLOPHONEUS 38 BRONTOPS 39 PROTOCERAS 40 million years ago 41

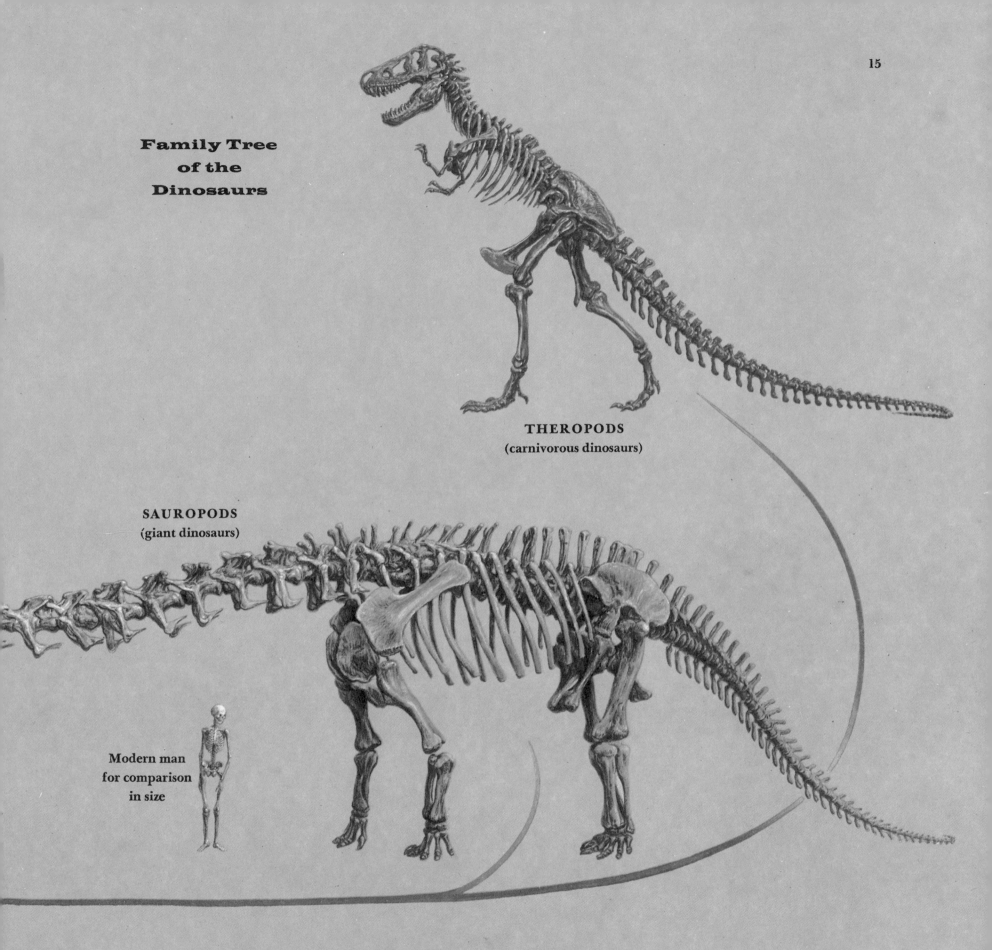

**Family Tree
of the
Dinosaurs**

THEROPODS
(carnivorous dinosaurs)

SAUROPODS
(giant dinosaurs)

Modern man
for comparison
in size

SAURISCHIAN DINOSAURS

HYRACHYUS

42

UINTATHERIUM

43

44

MESONYX

45

46

TRITEMNODON

47

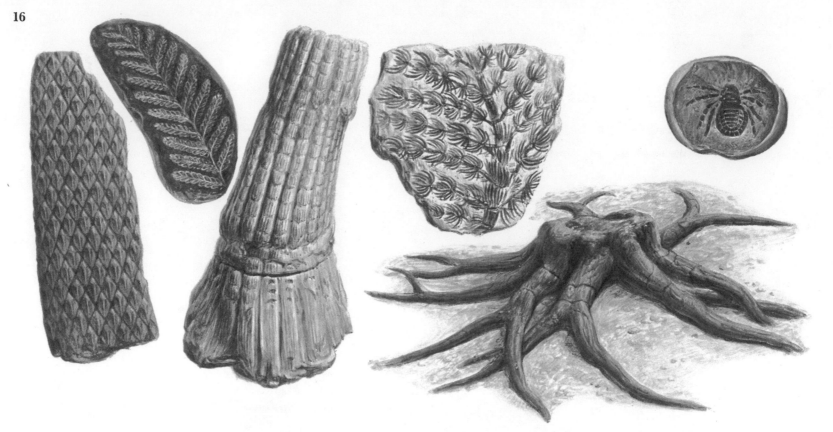

Fossils of plants and insect of the Carboniferous Period

THE SWAMPY WOODLAND

250 Million Years Ago in the Carboniferous Period

LET US take a look at the world of 250 million years ago.

Not a house, not a road, not a person do we see. There are no human beings on earth.

All around is swampy woodland. The ground is covered with small green plants. Underneath, it is squishy and damp.

Above tower green, tree-like plants. Some are giant ferns. Some look rather like palms. But these are not the trees we know today.

The air is warm and damp and still. And the world seems strangely silent. We do not hear the chirp or twitter of a single bird. We do not see the flutter of a feathered wing. There are no birds in the world.

In all the moist greenery we do not see a single flower. These plants do not have blossoms to produce their seeds. There are no flowers in this world.

We do not see many small, busy animals hurrying about. The small animals we know are mostly mammals. They had not yet appeared in this world of 250 million years ago.

Look! There is something moving. It looks like a bird, a big one, too. As we look more closely, we see that it has wings more than two feet across. But they are not feathered. They shimmer like glass. It is no bird but a giant dragonfly that we see.

There are insects aplenty in the world, some of the same kinds we know today. We see a cobweb in the sunlight, hung with heavy drops of dew. So there are spiders. And scuttling underfoot are scorpions, cockroaches and many-footed millipedes.

Swampy woodland of the Carboniferous Period

SALTOPOSUCHUS   PHYTOSAUR   PROCOMPSOGNATHUS

THE FIRST OF THE DINOSAURS

180 Million Years Ago in the Triassic Period

SH! We hear a rustling in the greenery and a soft sound of running feet. A swift, small figure crosses the clearing.

We have a view of long legs on a small, smooth body, We see a long, thin tail whipping out behind. A pointed head on a long, thin neck turns this way and that, hunting for big juicy bugs.

This is Procompsognathus, an early meat-eating dinosaur. But how small it is! Procompsognathus is not much bigger than a good-sized turkey would be, stripped of its feathers and given a long, thin tail.

This is not our idea of a dinosaur. We expect them to be huge and powerful. But it took many millions of years for the dinosaurs to develop giants among them. Many of the early ones were quite small.

Sunning himself nearby is Phytosaur. He looks like a crocodile. But he is a thecodont reptile. By the end of the Triassic Period his kind had disappeared.

There is another reptile now, the one with dark stripes like the rungs on a ladder down its back. Saltoposuchus is its name.

  60  61 million years ago 62  63 64 

PHENACODUS   OXYAENA   BARYLAMBDA   PANTOLAMBDA

PLATEOSAURUS

It stands, when on its hind feet, about three feet tall. But it is really longer than that, from nose-tip to tail. For it does not stand up straight, as we do. It leans forward as it runs.

Saltoposuchus is a good example of the pre-dinosaur "teeth-in-sockets." It can run fast on its light, bird-like feet. It looks rather like a large lizard. Saltoposuchus is small enough to hide from bigger hunters. It has big eyes for finding smaller animals. It can catch them in sharp claws and tear them with sharp teeth set in strong jaws. Saltoposuchus is well built to take care of itself.

Procompsognathus is a meat-eater too. And he has found a meal. As he bends down, reaching with tiny forearms, we see what the meal is. It is a nest of big, pale-colored eggs.

What animals can lay such big eggs? We wonder.

We learn the answer soon enough. For here comes the mother. She does not usually look after her eggs, once they are laid. But she is not pleased to see this small hunter digging them out of their warm, moist nest of grasses. She stamps and threshes her long tail. And Procompsognathus runs.

The giant mother is Plateosaurus, Flat Lizard. She does not look flat to us! She must be twenty feet long from nose to tail. Her small head waves high atop her long neck. And her eyes look wild.

Plateosaurus was the giant of the early days of dinosaurs. Like Saltoposuchus and Procompsognathus, she was reptile-hipped. She ran on her hind legs. But when she fed on green plants, she rested on her strong fore-limbs as well.

She was mainly a plant-eater. But her small relatives took no chances. They hid from her sight.

ORNITHOLESTES

ARCHAEOPTERYX

END OF MESOZOIC ERA, Time of the Dinosaurs

72 million years ago

73

74

75

76

STRUTHIOMIMUS

TRICERATOPS

Fossil remains of Archaeopteryx

THE WARM, WIDE SEAS

150 Million Years Ago in the Jurassic Period

ALL AROUND we hear the soft slosh of water against the shores. The waters of earth have risen. Shallow lakes and seas now cover much of what we know today as Europe and North America.

The sunshine beats down. Mist hangs over the water. The climate is warm and sticky. But plant life is doing very well. All around tower palms and huge, fern-like trees. Under them grows a tangle of green.

This is a time when plants which are found only in the tropics today grew almost to the North Pole. All over the earth, the climate is mild.

In the treetops we see the movement of a bird's wing. Surely it is a bird! It does not soar through the air. Instead, it seems to pull itself along in the trees, with the help of claws on its wings. And now and then it glides across an open space.

This is "Ancient Wing" or Archaeopteryx, the first true bird. It is about the size of the pigeons we see today.

Archaeopteryx still has some scales on its legs. For, like all birds, it developed from a reptile. But most of the scales have been replaced by light feathers. It still has a long, reptile tail. But the tail has feathers which help the bird to glide.

Not far away in the woods another small form flaps from tree to tree. This is "Ancient Bird" or Archaeornis. It is very, very similar to Archaeopteryx. Perhaps it is, in fact, the same.

These birds are light and swift-moving. They need to be. For there are many hungry hunters in the woods.

Here comes a swift dinosaur on the hunt. It is called Bird Stealer, Ornitholestes. Bird Stealer is about five feet long with a light body and long legs. It can run lightly on its two pronged feet. It can move very swiftly in the shadows. And it has long clutching fingers on its short forelegs. They are strong enough to snatch a bird from its perch. That is why men have given it this name.

78   79   80   81   82   83

STYRACOSAURUS   MONOCLONIUS

RHAMPHORHYNCHUS

OUT OVER the water, safe from Bird Stealer's reach, flies another creature. This is Prow Beak or Rhamphorhynchus. Prow Beak is not really a bird but a flying reptile. Instead of feathers it has a leathery skin.

Prow Beak's body is very small and light. Its bones are hollow. It has a long, sharp-beaked head and a long tail. But most important are its hands. One bony finger of each hand has grown very, very long. It supports a sheet of skin attached the whole length of the lizard's body. When Prow Beak raises his arms, these two sheets of skin become a pair of wings for gliding. He can really fly too. So his heart probably pumps warm blood through his body, though most reptiles are cold-blooded.

Prow Beak even has a sort of rudder on the end of his tail to help him steer. See! He glides down to the water, steering with the disk on the end of his tail. His large teeth grip a slippery fish. And away he goes.

84 million years ago   85   86   87   88

GORGOSAURUS   TRACHODON   CORYTHOSAURUS

We would like to see how he perches when he comes to rest. For scientists do not know whether Rhamphorhynchus used his feet, as birds do today, or hung by the "hands" on his wings. But we will not find out this time. For he disappears from sight.

As Prow Beak flies away, a pointed nose pokes up from the sea. It looks like a huge fish with a mouthful of sharp teeth. But really it is a reptile. This is Fish Lizard, or Ichthyosaurus. He is a reptile that went back to the sea to live. His feet turned into firm flippers. His long, thin lizard tail fanned out like a fish tail. His body became streamlined like that of a fish.

But Fish Lizards are not really fish. They still breathe air with lungs and have no fish gills. And the female does not lay eggs as a female fish does.

Instead the mother ichthyosaur keeps her eggs inside her own body. She hatches them safely there. Her babies are born alive, and live in the sea all their lives. They get along so well in the sea that some of them grow to be 40 feet long!

Another reptile which has gone back to the sea is the Geosaurus. This inappropriate name means Earth Lizard. These reptiles are also called marine crocodiles. They are related to the crocodiles we know. But their four short legs have turned into paddles. They paddle through the water. And they push themselves along with their tails, as fishes do. They live all their lives in water. They never go ashore any more, it seems, except to lay their eggs.

ICHTHYOSAURUS

GEOSAURUS

90   91   92   93   94   95

LAMBEOSAURUS   PARASAUROLOPHUS   PACHYCEPHALOSAURUS   ANKLYOSAURUS

FAR INLAND, up a river, where the water is fairly shallow, we see a strange sight. A pair of eyes and a pair of nostrils poke up above the still water. The bone around the nostrils forms a small dome. This dome belongs to Brachiosaurus, or Great Arms.

Great Arms is the heaviest of all dinosaurs. He weighs about fifty tons. As he thrusts his head up into the air, we see that he has a long, heavy neck. It is perched high on his heavy body. His huge front legs, or "arms," are longer and heavier than his back legs. They give him his name.

Brachiosaurus is so heavy that he needs four legs built like pillars to support his weight. But even they do not do it easily. This is one reason he stays in the water much of the time. The water helps hold him up.

The other reason is safety. Brachiosaurus is very slow-moving and clumsy when he does have to lumber out onto land. He could never run from an enemy. And he does not have much of a mind. His tiny brain weighs only a few ounces. It is not planned for quick reactions. So the safest thing to do is to hide.

Out in a quiet pool carpeted with water weeds, Brachiosaurus can eat and rest in peace. His neck is long enough to reach down to the bottom for greens. And his eyes are so arranged that he can keep a watch on things without being seen.

BRACHIOSAURUS

96   million years ago   97   98   99   100   101

TYRANNOSAURUS   ELASMOSAURUS   TYLOSAURUS

102　　BRACHAUCHENIUS　　103　　　　　　　104　　ICHTHYOSAURUS　　105　　　　　　　106　　ARCHELON　　107

Near by feeds Diplodocus, whose name means the Double Beamed. He is the longest of all dinosaurs. He measures as much as 87½ feet. But he is more lightly and slimly built than Brachiosaurus.

If Diplodocus does have to go ashore, he walks with his long neck stretching far out in front to balance the long tail behind.

But Diplodocus does not waste much time walking. For his head and mouth are tiny. His body is huge. He can take only very small bites with his weak teeth. And it takes a lot to make a meal for him.

So Diplodocus has to spend most of his time steadily eating to keep himself well fed.

DIPLODOCUS

Cretaceous Period

| 114 | IGUANODON | 115 | PROTOCERATOPS | 116 | | 117 | PSITTACOSAURUS | 118 | 119 |

ALLOSAURUS

BRONTOSAURUS

120 million years ago   121   122   123   124   125

ORNITHOLESTES   ALLOSAURUS

The third dinosaur giant is Brontosaurus, Thunder Lizard. Thunder Lizard does not go ashore much either. Like the two other giants, she is a peace-loving plant-eater. She is not as heavy as Brachiosaurus, nor as long as Diplodocus. But she does weigh thirty tons. And she is 67 feet long from nose to tail tip. So she too is most comfortable in the water, with the weight off her feet.

Today Brontosaurus has come ashore to lay some eggs. She has just finished smoothing sand and grasses over the nestful. Then she heads back for the safety of the water. But today is not her lucky day. Allosaurus the hunter has caught sight of her!

Allosaurus is not interested in eggs. And he does not care for plants to eat. He likes meat—great chunks of fresh meat! He is big—35 feet long.

Allosaurus has sharp claws at the ends of his short forelegs. They can get a grip and really hold on. His teeth are big and sharp. And he has a tremendous appetite.

Standing on his hind legs, Allosaurus balances himself by leaning on his muscular tail. And he watches Brontosaurus lumbering along, heading for the safety of the water.

Allosaurus blows out his breath in a great snort and takes off after his prey. Just at the shore he leaps.

What a battle this is! Allosaurus sinks his sharp claws into Brontosaurus's meaty shoulder. But the plant-eater whips around her great tail and knocks the hunter back.

Brontosaurus plunges out into shallow water. And Allosaurus strikes again. His jaws close upon her neck. Brontosaurus cannot save herself now. But as she sinks, she throws her great weight upon the killer. Allosaurus, with his jaws still locked about Bronto's neck, is pushed beneath the water. Thirty tons pin him, helpless, in the sand.

Up the shore Camptosaurus, Bent Lizard, lifts his head from a meal of fresh-water plants. He rears up on his hind legs to watch.

But soon the water rolls peacefully over the hidden forms. Slowly a layer of shifting sand blankets killer and victim alike.... And so the years roll on.

CAMPTOSAURUS

STEGOSAURUS

132 million years ago   133   134   135   136   137

DIPLODOCUS   BRACHIOSAURUS

ANKYLOSAURUS

THE FLOWERING LAND

120 Million Years Ago in the Cretaceous Period

WHAT a change has come upon the earth! The air feels fresher and cooler. It is not moist and sticky now. We are not surrounded by swamps and seas any more. Here we see a rolling country with woods of oak and hickory. Down in the hollows where the streams run, we see the pale green of willows. And through the shadowy woods we catch glimpses of flowers. For flowering plants have appeared!

Flowering plants are new in the world. And there is a new sound to go with them. It is a familiar sound to us. It is the buzzing of bees. Bees began their work of spreading flower pollen way back here, 120 million years ago. They are still busy at it today.

There are dinosaurs here too. But some of the old giants have died out. Brontosaurus, Diplodocus, Brachiosaurus all have vanished. As the wide, shallow waters dwindled, perhaps there was not enough green plant food left to feed all these hungry giants. So through the ages fewer of them grew up. They laid fewer eggs. And at last there were none at all.

New groups of dinosaurs, whose bodies are protected, appear now. They cannot run rapidly for protection from hunters. So they have developed their own protection. These dinosaurs wear coats of armor.

An early armored dinosaur which lived in the Jurassic Period was Stegosaurus, Covered Lizard. The tall, stiff armor plates standing up from his high-curved, 20-foot-long back looked hard to bite. And no one wanted that tail with its sharp two-foot spikes swung at him. So most enemies left Stegosaurus alone.

All the armored dinosaurs were bird-hipped, including Stegosaurus. His hind legs were long and strong. His hip bones were firmly fitted to his backbone. And, though he walked on all fours, his front legs were short, as with most bird-hips.

New armored dinosaurs are seen now. Ankylosaurus or Curved Lizard is one. His name comes from his curved ribs. He has a wide, flat body. His back is covered with thick plates of bone. His legs are short, and he is built low to the ground. As he walks through the woods, he looks almost like a giant horned toad.

All around the edge of his armor coat he wears a set of long spikes. They stand out straight. They do not look tasty to a hunter. His long tail has a heavy knot on the end. He can swing this tail like a club. So most meat-eating dinosaurs leave him alone.

IGUANODON

HERE WE ARE back at a swampy shore. For there still are great swamps and lakes and seas in the world. Along the shores still live many dinosaurs. These are not the huge, reptile-hipped giants of old. These are a newer, bird-hipped family, the duck-bills.

The first of this sort, though not truly a duck-bill, was Camptosaurus or Bent Lizard. We saw him, you remember, back twenty million years or more. Then he was quietly chomping water plants with his horny-beaked bill. And he managed to stay out of reach of the giant hunters. For, being only five to eight feet tall, his kind was no match for the giants.

Now an age has passed. The giants of old have vanished. But a relative of Camptosaurus, Iguanodon, is still around, still chomping away. His name means Lizard Tooth. He has grown much larger than Bent Lizard. This one must be thirty feet long. He has a specially thick, heavy tail and a spike on his thumb.

He has other good points too. He can walk on either two feet or four. This is handy. He has webbed feet, like ducks of today. They make it easy for him to walk over soft, wet ground. These may be some of the reasons his kind have lived on from age to age.

A later relative of Iguanodon is duck-billed Trachodon or Rough Tooth. He comes swimming easily in to shore. His heavy tail sweeps the water behind him. As he wallows ashore, he rears up on his hind legs. And he leans back to balance on his tail. Now we see that he too is much larger than Bent Lizard.

Trachodon shakes the water from his leathery skin and opens wide his flat, broad, duck-bill jaws. With these jaws Trachodon probably can eat plants that grow under water, just as can the dabbling ducks we know today. Now we see why he was given his name. Look at those teeth! A thousand teeth pave his lower jaw like a rough cobblestone street. A thousand more in his upper jaw help grind Rough Tooth's meals of water plants. He has more teeth than any other reptile.

TRACHODON

All the duck-bills stay near the water. They waddle along the shores, now on two feet, again on four. Some of them prefer to be in the water. And some even like to stay under it!

How do they manage to stay under water? They really do not breathe there. They have special air storage spaces built into their skulls. These bones look like crested caps or helmets from the outside.

But inside are hollow spaces to hold a small supply of air. This structure keeps water out of the windpipe while the animal feeds under water. Let's see how it works.

Two of these duck-bills are on the shore. One is Corythosaurus whose bony head looks as if he were wearing a helmet. The other is Parasaurolophus who has a bony crest on his head.

GORGOSAURUS

Here comes danger! The danger is Gorgosaurus, a giant hunter. He belongs to the family of old Allosaurus. But he is larger still. And he is hungry most of the time.

Corythosaurus, the Helmet Lizard, and Parasaurolophus, Like-a-Crested-Lizard, see their danger.

They race for the water. Out they splash, deeper and deeper. As they swim on the surface they take deep breaths. They fill their hollow skulls with air. And down they go to the bottom. There they can feed for a little while, safely out of reach. That is a good way to escape dangers on the shore.

CORYTHOSAURUS   **PARASAUROLOPHUS**

PSITTACOSAURUS

FROM THE PLAINS OF MONGOLIA
TO THE UPLANDS OF NORTH AMERICA

100 to 90 Million Years Ago

ON the high open plains a new family has become large and successful. This family is the horned dinosaurs. They have come a long way since the day of their ancestor Psittacosaurus, seen above.

Psittacosaurus is a strange little fellow. He has a sharp, pointed beak, shaped something like a parrot's beak. So the scientists, who found his bones in the Gobi Desert, call him Parrot Lizard. He does not look like much of a dinosaur to us. But wait and see what his family develops into! For Parrot Lizard is the great grandfather of the horned dinosaurs, the last of the great dinosaur families.

On the next page we see one of the first of these horned dinosaurs. Men call him Protoceratops or First Horned Face. He lived on the dry plains of Mongolia. He is not very large, perhaps six or eight feet long. A family often starts out small and grows larger through the ages. That is what the horned dinosaurs did.

Protoceratops is quite fierce-looking, though. For back of his parrot beak he wears a wide, bony cap. It stands out fiercely around his face.

To be sure, Protoceratops does not have horns. But his parrot beak and the long frill of bones which goes from the back of his skull out over his neck show that he is an ancestor of all the horned dinosaurs that appeared later.

Protoceratops walks on all four of his legs. But his front legs are shorter than his hind legs. At some long distant time in the past, his forefathers may possibly have walked on only their hind legs.

Tasty meals of green plants are all the food that Protoceratops ever eats. Most of the time he can chomp away without being disturbed. For the

PROTOCERATOPS

meat-eating dinosaurs of his day have learned that sturdy Protoceratops can put up a good fight if he has to, so they usually leave him alone.

Look at the ground here. A female Protoceratops has laid a nestful of eggs in a sandy hollow. The eggs look very large to us. Each egg is about eight inches long. The shell and the shape of the shell looks almost like turtle eggs we would find in our own time.

Watch! One egg, then another begins to quiver and crack. They are ready to hatch. The first baby crawls out. It has no bony cap as yet. That will come as it grows up. Now it is just very small and weak. And from the looks of things, it may not live to grow up. For here comes a hungry hunter.

The hunter is very small for a dinosaur, only about three feet long. Although he is hungry, meat is not the kind of meal he wants, for he has no

Jurassic Period

168 million years ago   169   170   171   172   173

PLATEOSAURUS   CYNOGNATHUS

OVIRAPTOR

teeth. Sucking eggs is his idea of a feast. This is why scientists of today call him Oviraptor which means Egg Stealer. If he cannot find eggs, he will make do with fruits and other soft foods.

But today he has found a banquet, a whole nest of eggs. They are ready to hatch. Perhaps Oviraptor could manage to eat a soft-boned, newly hatched Protoceratops. We cannot be sure. Because he does not have time to eat this meal.

The sky darkens. A cold wind rises. The wind sends stones rattling across the ground. It sends clouds of sand rolling and tumbling. Oviraptor feels the sting of the needle-like sand grains. He crouches on the nest, hiding his head. The sand slithers along. It piles up, drifting over the nest and eggs. It drifts over Oviraptor too.

The wind dies down. The sand settles. And now the desert is bare of life.

GORGOSAURUS

STYRACOSAURUS

ACROSS THE OCEAN in a distant land which we now know as North America, we find more horned dinosaurs of a somewhat later time.

Here, coming upon them too, is Gorgosaurus. We know him as the Terrible Lizard. He can smell meat near by. So he is stamping about, looking for it.

First he comes face to face with Styracosaurus, or Spike Lizard. And what a face this is to meet! A long, sharp horn tilts upward from Spike Lizard's parrot-beaked nose. But that is not all. He wears a great frill of horn standing up on his head. And the frill is decked with sharp spikes all along its edge.

Gorgosaurus strides forward. Spike Lizard's watchful eyes follow every step. He moves his sharp horn slowly from side to side.

Before that threat Gorgosaurus weakens. His hide already bears the scars of that sharp horn. He wants no more of it. Snuffling with rage, he backs and turns away.

Next he meets Monoclonius, or Single Horn. Monoclonius is big enough to make a good meal.

But there are other things to consider. The "single horn" for which this dinosaur is named is long and sharp. It grows from his nose.

As Monoclonius stands with his great head lowered, that sharp horn is tilted straight at Terrible Lizard. Above Monoclonius' eyes small horns glint in the sunlight. Gorgosaurus decides he is not hungry enough to tackle this horned giant either. He moves on, hungry still.

MONOCLONIUS

TRICERATOPS

PTERANODON

THE LAST OF THE GIANTS

70 Million Years Ago

THE EARTH has been changing again. Slowly, slowly, huge sections of land have been pushed up, up. Once, millions of years before, they had lain at the bottom of a shallow sea. Now they have been pushed far above the waters. The seas have shrunk back. Some of these lands are now high, dry plains.

In other places huge sheets of rock have been squeezed between other rocks. Through long ages they have been squeezed and squeezed. At the end of this era they will buckle and crack. They will crumple like a paper you crush in your hand. Instead of lying flat they will rise up into many high, sharp-peaked new mountains.

Far out at sea leathery-winged Pteranodon or Toothless Wing tilts his twenty-foot wings and glides with the wind. His big, sharp eyes scan the water below for food.

Pteranodon dips down and snatches a fish from the sea. On the ground he can move only awkwardly. His hind legs are small and weak. And he does not have much sense of smell.

Pteranodon is probably warm-blooded. Warm blood is a big advantage. His heart must pump very fast to keep him flying for long times as he hunts. But other reptiles are cold-blooded. They need sunlight and warmth to give them energy.

Back on land new warm-blooded animals are appearing. They are the furry mammals. They live mainly among the trees. For branches thick with leaves make good hiding places. And these small creatures must hide away to be safe.

A small mammal has come out hunting for insects and seeds. He wears a coat of fur. And his heart pumps warm blood through his body.

Nearby is Giant Triceratops, Three-Horn-Face, one of the cold-blooded dinosaurs. He sniffs the air unhappily. He moves his huge head from side to side. Six feet high that head towers with its immense frill of bone. Down close to the ground is his parrot-beak nose. Its small horn points straight ahead. Between his eyes are the other two horns which make him "Three-Horn-Face." They reach out three feet or more ahead. And their sharp points slice the air as Three-Horn moves his head.

BEGINNING OF MESOZOIC ERA
first of dinosaurs appear

END OF PALEOZOIC ERA, Time of Early Life

Triassic Period

| 198 | 199 | 200 | 201 | 202 | 203 |

DIMETRODON   EDAPHOSAURUS   OPHIACODON

From his nose to the end of his thick tail, Triceratops stretches between twenty and thirty feet long. His skull alone is five feet long, with its towering frill.

Three-Horn is not speedy. But his thick legs are full of power. He can lunge straight ahead like a bulldozer. And woe to anyone who gets in the path of those on-coming horns!

Who would dare face Triceratops? There is one hungry giant who will. This is meat-eating, roaring, snorting, tearing, slashing Tyrannosaurus, the Tyrant Lizard. Sometimes men add Rex or King to his name. For surely he must have been the ruler of his world. He was huge. He was powerful. He had to kill to live. And there were few creatures of his time he could not kill.

Here comes Tyrannosaurus now. He towers twenty feet tall as he pounds along on his clawed hind feet. His tail swishes heavily over the ground behind him. From head to tail he measures fifty feet—probably more than the length of your house!

Up at the height of a second-story window his great head sways. His head alone is longer than you are tall. Wide nostrils sniff for the smell of fresh meat. A huge mouth yawns like a dreadful red door. It is rimmed with teeth, each tooth six inches long and as sharp as a sword.

The thick skin hangs down from the Tyrant Lizard's neck in loose, empty folds. He has not had a good big meal for some time. But now he spies Triceratops. Those thick, meaty shanks would fill the Tyrant's huge stomach nicely!

Slowly, heavily he begins to circle around Three-Horn. He does not want to attack from the front because of those horns. He wants a bite at Three-Horn's unprotected side instead.

The Tyrant moves closer. Three-Horn stands firm. His horns are lowered for action. But unfortunately for him his mind does not work fast. While Three-Horn just stands there, Tyrant Lizard circles a clump of bushes—and lunges!

A heavy-clawed hind foot rips Three-Horn's flank. The Tyrant's sword-sharp teeth reach for Three-Horn's windpipe.

But Three-Horn has not lost the fight. Not yet! He has special weapons for defense. His skull is balanced on a handy ball-and-socket joint below his bony frill. And attached to the bottom of that bony frill are huge and powerful neck muscles. His leg muscles are very powerful too. Putting all these muscles and joints to work, Three-Horn manages to turn under the Tyrant's attack. He lunges sideways. And he catches the Tyrant in the ribs with those two sharp horns of his! There is a thunder-sharp crack of snapping bones! With a roar of rage and pain, the Tyrant rears back. His small foreclaws flail at Three-Horn. But he does not want to risk another jab from those horns.

Three-Horn just stands there. He may not be smart. But he can look after himself.

With another roar, Tyrant Lizard shuffles away to rest and lick his wounds. He is really tired. Like all cold-blooded animals, he tires quickly. And this has been a hard day for him.

TYRANNOSAURUS

PACHYCEPHALOSAURUS

NEXT DAY, down along the sunny shore, Tyrant Lizard finds the hunting better. He can walk fairly fast on his two legs on dry land. But he does not like to get too close to the water. For he weighs eight tons or more. His clawed feet sink deep in soft mud or sand. He may get stuck completely. At best he is slowed down.

But sometimes the duck-billed dinosaurs along the shore come back onto dry ground. That is what Tyrant Lizard is hoping for. Duck-bills are big enough to make a good meal. And they do not have sharp horns and spikes.

Or do they? There is Lambeosaurus now. And on his head he wears a crest shaped like a double-bladed hatchet. This crest has hollow bones to hold air.

Lambeosaurus can hide under water for some time, though Tyrant Lizard does not know that. He does seem to know that the crest will not harm him.

Hungrily the Tyrant watches Lambeosaurus. Soon the duck-bill walks away over the sand on

Here comes Pachycephalosaurus, Thick-Headed Lizard. He belongs to a group of rather small dinosaurs related to the duck-bills.

Pachycephalosaurus has a small brain. But he has good protection for it. His brain is protected by a dome of solid skull bone nine inches thick! And the outside of his head is decorated with extra bumps and points of bone.

LAMBEOSAURUS

his broad, webbed feet. Then out into the water he goes. And he drops to all four feet for a lunch of water plants.

Tyrannosaurus swishes his tail angrily. He cannot follow Lambeosaurus there. And he is getting impatient, and hungrier still. But he does not have much longer to wait.

Tyrant Lizard does not care about that thick skull. He does not mind the bony bumps on Thick Head's face. They cannot hurt him. He is interested in Thick Head's plumpness. He is interested in food. So he lunges with tooth and claw!

Down goes Pachycephalosaurus. And Tyrant Lizard has a good meal at last.

RIDING THE SWELLS of this broad inland sea is a bird. It seems very large to us. For it is more than four feet long. It is Hesperornis or Western Bird. Off in the distance float more of the same kind. They look much like the loons which swim on our lakes of today.

Now and then we see one dive for a fish. But as long as we may watch, we shall never see one fly. For these are birds which have lost their power of flight. Through ages of living on the sea, their wings have almost disappeared. Now they are far too small to support Hesperornis in flight.

So Hesperornis cannot fly. It cannot even walk or stand. For its webbed paddle feet on short legs are set way at the back of its body. It could not keep its balance if it tried to stand on those legs.

On water, though, Hesperornis is completely at home. It swims very well. The feet are just right for that. And its sharp teeth can snatch plenty of fishes for food. So Hesperornis gets along nicely at sea.

There are plenty of fishes in these waters. Fishes have lived on since before the days of reptiles and amphibians. They were the first creatures to have

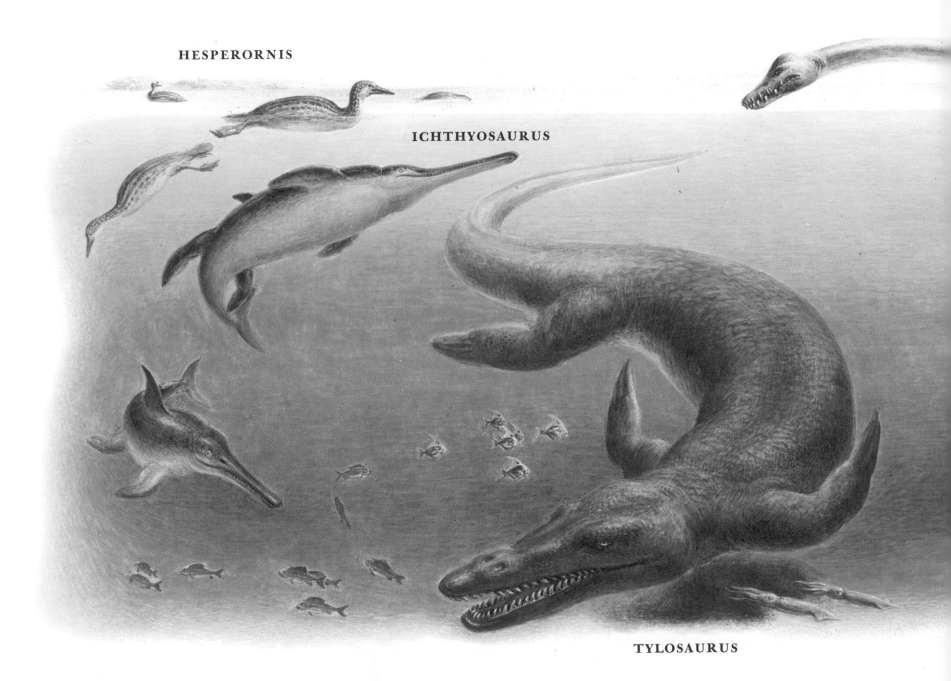

HESPERORNIS

ICHTHYOSAURUS

TYLOSAURUS

skeletons made of bone. And most of the families we know today—the herring, the swordfish, the sturgeon and pike, the sharks (whose skeletons are made of cartilage instead of bone) and others— were already swimming ancient seas as long ago as Cretaceous times.

But there are also "reptiles" of the seas. These are reptiles which, like the bird Hesperornis, have lost their ability to live on land. They live in the sea instead.

Ichthyosaurus, the Fish Lizard, has been swimming the oceans of the world since back in Triassic times. (We saw a member of his family in the world of 150 million years ago.) But Ichthyosaurus is not the only one.

Near by, Elasmosaurus or Thin-Plate Lizard rows himself peacefully along. His long, paddle-shaped limbs serve as oars. They move with slow, smooth strokes. For Elasmosaurus is not in a hurry.

There is no need for speed. His flat, broad body is not built for it. His head moves fast enough. On his long, thin neck his head can dart swiftly this way and that. He can reach out twenty feet in any direction. He can surprise a lot of fish!

ELASMOSAURUS

Elasmosaurus is forty feet long. And much of that length is in his snake-like neck. In fact one early scientist described him as "a snake drawn through the body of a turtle." His body is really not too different in size from that of twelve-foot Archelon, the Ruler Turtle of the seas.

At the end of his snaky neck, Elasmosaurus has jaws full of long, sharp-pointed teeth. They can snap swiftly shut on a swimming fish.

Also he has such strong leg muscles that he can paddle backward as well as ahead. So Elasmosaurus does not go hungry, even though he may not be swift.

Elasmosaurus is just one member of the Plesiosaur, or Near-Lizard, family. Another is Trinacromerum. He has a shorter neck and a larger jaw. He is in the picture below along with Archelon.

His legs have turned to flippers too. But the bones in them are still strong enough so that Trinacromerum, like many other members of his family, can go ashore if he wishes. And he can pull himself about there as seals do on rocky beaches today.

See the wild-looking giant with Elasmosaurus. This is Tylosaurus, a twenty-footer of the Mosasaur family. Tylosaurus, as you can see, is not as sleek and fish-like as Ichthyosaurus. But, like Ichthyosaurus, it does swish along through the water by side-wise motions of its body and tail. It swims like a fish. And it uses its paddle-like limbs just to keep its balance in the water. What gives it a wild and dangerous look is its huge, tooth-filled jaws.

Mosasaurs are called sea lizards. And they really are lizards which went back to the sea to live. They get along so well in the sea that they have grown to be giant sea-serpents. They are the size of some of our whales of today.

ARCHELON   **TRINACROMERUM**

EARLY OPOSSUMS

TYRANNOSAURUS

END OF AN ERA

Close of the Cretaceous Period, End of the Age of Reptiles

THE WORLD is changing. Dry plains are rising up where, not long ago, quiet shallow seas lapped softly at their shores. Hardwood forests tower in place of tender ferns and palms.

This new world is no place for dinosaurs. As the swamps shrink, their food supply dwindles. And they have not the brains to figure out how to find new foods. Among the close-growing trees of the new forests, they cannot move easily. So the last of the giants wander sadly. At last they sink down, many of them weakened by disease or hunger.

The small, furry mammals are growing in size and numbers. They are beginning to spread over the world. Mammals like the shelter of the new forests. The first of their kind have been hiding in tree branches for many millions of years. This is a good world for them.

The mammals have bigger brains, too, than the dinosaurs. They can figure out how to get food. And, once in a while, the food they find themselves may be dinosaur eggs. Or they may even feast on a fallen giant himself.

Mammals eating dinosaur eggs

So the mammals prosper. Their great day is dawning. (The day of the mammals is still going on. We are living in it. We are mammals too.)

Meanwhile the dinosaurs die off, often leaving no eggs or young behind them. One by one, whole families vanish. The horned beasts of the high country are the last to go. But as the period of time we call the Cretaceous slips slowly into the past, every dinosaur has vanished from the earth.

No longer does the ground shake under the heavy tramp of Tyrannosaurus rex. No more do broad-winged flying lizards flap across the skies. They have vanished too. Even the great lizards in the seas have vanished. No more do the Mosasaurs and Plesiosaurs and Ichthyosaurs snap at passing fish. They seemed perfectly suited to their life. It seemed that nothing could stop them. But, with their great cousins the dinosaurs, the swimming reptiles vanished mysteriously from the world.

Oh, there are a few reptiles which live on. Crocodiles and alligators still slither along in tropical streams. Lizards, built a bit like miniature dinosaurs, still drowse on rocks in the sun. Turtles still go their quiet way, much as they did almost 200 million years ago.

Birds, which developed from reptiles, still swoop and soar across our skies. But not a dinosaur do we see. No man has ever seen a living dinosaur. For, long millions of years before the first man lived, the day of the dinosaurs was done.

Reptiles of Today

ALLIGATOR

TURTLE

LIZARD

SNAKE

Mary Anning found a fossil Ichthyosaurus.

DINOSAUR HUNTING

From 1800 to Today

FOR MANY millions of years, the dinosaurs were forgotten. Even 160 years ago, no one had ever heard of these huge and wonderful animals. There was not one in the world to be seen. How then did we ever find out about them?

Men learned about dinosaurs from fossils in rocks. It was a bit like learning to read. The rocks of earth are like a huge book. The rock layers are its pages. Hidden in them is the story of the earth's past. But to learn that story, men had to learn to read the book of the rocks.

In steep cliffs beside the sea, or in the straight-cut walls of a canal or stone quarry, men could see that rocks are piled up in layers. These layers differ in color and fineness. In general those lowest down are the oldest. As ages passed, other, newer layers

of rock were piled up on top of them, one by one.

In many layers seashells and bits of bone were packed tightly into the rock. These shells and bones found in rocks are called fossils.

Countless sea creatures have died and fallen to the bottom. Sometimes their shells broke up into powder-fine lime. They formed limestone. Other shells were covered with sand. As that sand was pressed into rock, the shells remained in the rock.

After ages more, the sea-bottom rocks were pushed up, up above the water to form new lands. And in those rocks the shells of ancient animals were hidden, waiting to tell us about themselves.

There are many other kinds of fossils, too. Any remains of long-gone, once-living things found in the rocks are called fossils.

There are fossils of leaves. A leaf may have fallen on soft ground, or into a shallow pond. More soft, muddy earth covered it, pressing it tight. As the leaf decayed, its outline was left pressed into the hard earth, which slowly changed to rock. Leaf fossils tell us what kinds of plants lived in each age.

Sometimes whole forests of fallen trees were buried and turned to stone. Of course this takes

long ages. Now these stone trees tell us how old they were when they fell and how large they grew.

Some fossils are footprints left in mud. Perhaps you have seen a sidewalk in which someone stepped before the concrete dried. As the concrete hardened like rock, the footprints stayed. They are like fossils.

From a set of footprints like that, a scientist could tell many things. He might say, "This person wore

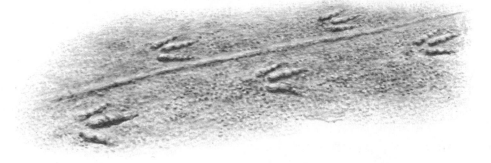

a size 11 shoe with a rubber sole. Judging from the length of his step, I should say he was nearly six feet tall. He stepped harder on his toes than on his heels. So probably he was running."

It is the same with the fossil trails of ancient animals. A farmer finds what look like huge footprints in the rocks of a pasture. He calls a scientist out to look at them. From these footprints alone, the scientist can say, "This was a big fellow. He walked on his hind feet. His feet were webbed, like a duck's, so he could walk easily across soft mud.

Perhaps this was a seashore ages ago. For here, near the footprints, is a fossil of a small sand crab."

Nowadays the scientist could probably even name the animal. He might say, "It was a duck-billed dinosaur, the Trachodon." But a hundred and fifty years ago, when a New England farmer did find some strange footprints in his field, no one had ever heard of dinosaurs. So of course there were no names for them.

It was a twelve-year-old girl in England who found the first whole fossil skeleton. It was not a dinosaur. But it was close.

The girl's name was Mary Anning. She and her family lived near the sea. She helped her father gather fossil seashells from the rocks. And they sold them to summer visitors to their town.

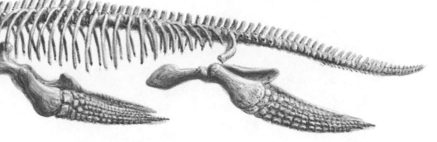

PLESIOSAURUS

One day in 1811, Mary found in the rocks the bones of a strange animal. It was a reptile which had lived in the sea. When it died its bones sank to the bottom and were buried in sand which turned to rock.

In a later age, that sea bottom rock was pushed up many feet. Part of it broke away, leaving a cliff.

We may wish the scientists had given these creatures easier names. But in those days the scientists of many lands wrote about their work in Latin or Greek. So they gave all these creatures Latin or Greek names. *Ichthys* is the old Greek word for fish. *Saurus* is the old Greek word for lizard. So what it really means is Fish Lizard.

Mary Anning found other bones too. In 1821 she found the first set of bones of a Plesiosaurus. Of course she did not know what it was. Scientists gave it that name after they put the bones together. They figured out from the bones how the animal had lived. They decided it was "nearly like a lizard." That is what its name means.

Mary was famous before she was grown up. But she kept on hunting fossils for many years. Some years later she found a pterodactyl, a reptile that could fly.

It was about this time too that an English lady, the wife of a physician, found some peculiar, large teeth in a rock. She took them home to her husband. He had never seen any like them. He asked other scientists about them. They made guesses. But no one really knew to what kind of animal those teeth had belonged.

The bones of the long-ago sea creature were left in the rock at the edge of the cliff. And there, millions of years later, Mary Anning found them.

Scientists had never seen bones like these before. The bones formed a perfect skeleton. Because it was like a fish, they called it Ichthyosaurus.

ICHTHYOSAURUS

So the wife took her husband back to the rock where she had found the teeth. He dug around and found a number of bones. He took the bones home and studied them. He decided they belonged to an unknown reptile. Because its teeth were like those of an iguana lizard, he named the newly discovered creature Iguanodon. But actually it was many years before a whole Iguanodon skeleton was found so that people could really see how he had looked. And he did not look much like an iguana lizard after all.

We know that Iguanodon was a duck-billed dinosaur. We met him and a cousin of his, Trachodon, on pages 32 and 33. Another cousin, Hadrosaurus, was the first dinosaur to be found in North America. Some of his bones were turned up in a clay pit near Philadelphia. It was many years before a scientist got a look at those bones. For the workmen gave away those they found to friends. But finally most of them were gathered together. More were dug up. And the 25-foot-long fellow was given the name of Hadrosaurus or Bulky Lizard.

As the bones of more of these huge reptiles were found, one scientist decided there should be a name for all of them. He decided to call them "the terrible lizards," or dinosauria.

And now the dinosaur hunters really went to work, looking for still more new kinds.

As explorers began to scout around the Wild West, in the years after the Civil War, they sent back word of strange bones they found. Soon many parties of scientists and helpers were going west on fossil hunts. And they found rich hunting grounds.

Out in Wyoming they found a skeleton of Brontosaurus. The great backbone was bitten through. Some of the bones had tooth marks in them. There were even broken teeth of the killer among the bones. The scientists checked those teeth. They measured those tooth marks. Both belonged to Allosaurus. So they knew that the hunter Allosaurus had been strong enough to kill the huge plant-eater Brontosaurus, as we saw on pages 28 and 29.

It took the hunters six months to take out the bones of Brontosaurus. Another dinosaur hunter had an even harder job. He found a skeleton of Tyrannosaurus. This was in the bad lands of Montana. What a time he had with that skeleton!

The rock around the skeleton was very, very hard. The scientists even had to use dynamite to tear down parts of the hill above it. They worked two summers getting those bones out, in blocks of sandstone. Then they had to haul the huge blocks by wagon to the railroad more than a hundred miles away.

HADROSAURUS

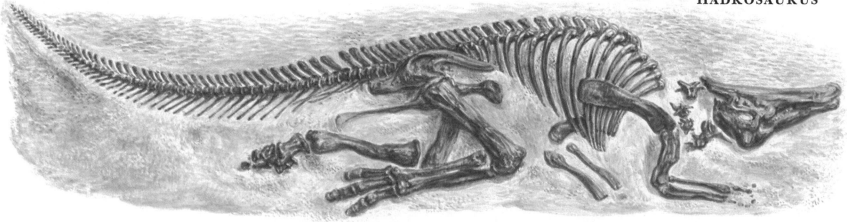

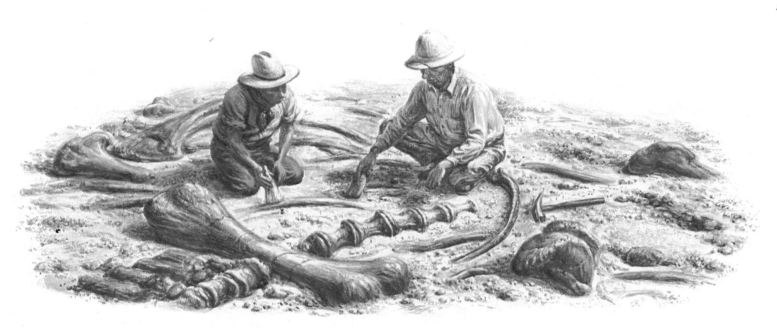

Scientists cleaning fossils found on a field trip.

Good country for dinosaur hunting usually has lots of bare rock. Where soil and grass and trees have gathered over the rocks, you cannot see the bones sticking out. These lands with bare rock are often deserts. They have very hot summers. And it is hard to find food. So dinosaur hunters have to be real explorers. They have to be willing to camp out and live in rough spots.

Dinosaur hunters have traveled by boat, by train, by wagon. They have ridden on horses, mules, camels, even on elephants!

They travel any way they can to reach an area where there is bare rock of the right kind to contain the fossils they want.

Then they begin to hunt with care. They study the distant land with field glasses. They scramble up steep cliffs. They pick their way along rocky ravines. They float down rivers in small boats, keeping sharp eyes on the rocky walls. They walk long, thirsty miles under broiling sun.

Whenever they see a piece of tell-tale bone, they really go to work. Sometimes they use pick axes. Other times they use whisk brooms to keep from harming a delicate bone. And often, when they get back home, the bones fit together to form an animal no one has ever seen before!

One group of hunters, far off on the Gobi Desert in Asia, even found nests of dinosaur eggs. Some had tiny unborn dinosaurs inside.

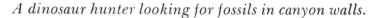

A dinosaur hunter looking for fossils in canyon walls.

On top of one nest they found the bones of a small dinosaur which had been sucking eggs for its dinner when a great sandstorm came swirling along. We met (on page 36) the female dinosaur, Protoceratops which had laid these eggs. We also saw Oviraptor which had invaded the nest.

The small thief and the eggs were buried together, perhaps under many feet of sand. And there they stayed for millions of years. But slowly the sand shifted again. So by the time our hunters came along, parts of the eggs could be seen.

All around that desert area the hunters found dinosaur eggs. They decided that ages ago, great numbers of dinosaurs had come to that place to lay their eggs. Some of the sandy nests were buried so deep by windstorms that the eggs never hatched.

The sand on top of the eggs cracked the shells. The liquid inside ran out. Sand sifted in to fill the space. Slowly the sand inside and outside was pressed into rock. And there were the eggs, just the same shape as when they had been laid. But now they were as heavy as stone. For they were filled with rock inside!

You may say, "Why can't we go dinosaur hunting today?"

You can. There are many places where countless bones are waiting to be found. Montana, Utah, Wyoming, Colorado and other parts of the West have many dinosaur skeletons still. Kansas was once at the bottom of a huge inland sea. Hundreds of huge sea reptiles have been found in chalk layers there. More are waiting to be found.

Fossils have been found on every continent. They have been found in deep mines, in peaceful river valleys, along sea coasts, on dry deserts. And there are many, many areas which have never been explored for them. Hidden away in the sandy rocks laid down in the Triassic, Jurassic and Cretaceous Ages are countless bones. Some may be of animals we do not know today. Many have been waiting for more than a hundred million years. You may be the one to find them there!

Covering dinosaur bones with a plaster cast.

HOW TO HANDLE A DINOSAUR

AFTER you have located your dinosaur, there is still a lot of work to do. Usually only a few bones can be seen poking out from the rock at the edge of a cliff. The rest of the skeleton is buried. Sometimes there are tons and tons of rock on top of it. All this rock must be moved away.

This is often a long, slow, hot and tiresome job. With pick and shovel the ground must be loosened and loaded into wagons or carts for hauling away.

Finally you work down to the level of the fossil dinosaur. At this stage you must be very careful lest the point of your pick smash into a bone.

Taking dinosaur bones in a plaster block down a bluff.

Back in the laboratory rocks are cleaned from a fossil skull.

A supporting iron frame is attached to the fossil skull.

Smaller tools are used now—perhaps a sharp awl driven in with a small hammer, perhaps a whisk broom or brush.

As soon as one side of a bone has been laid bare, it must be protected from the air and against the shock of sudden movement. For these fossil bones are very fragile. Just as soon as the bone comes to light, it is given a coat of shellac and is covered with soft paper.

Then when it is ready to be removed from the rock, it is put in a sort of "cast," like a broken arm or leg. This cast is made of strips of burlap dipped in plaster. It is laid over the top of the bones and allowed to dry.

When one side of the fossil is protected by its cast, the other side is carefully separated from the rock. Then the whole thing is carefully turned over, cast side down and the other side gets its wet-plaster cast put on. Sometimes wooden splints are added to give extra strength.

Before the fossil is moved far, it is packed carefully in straw and strongly boxed for shipping to the museum.

In the museum, everything has to be undone. The crate must be opened, the straw carefully removed, the fossil in its burlap cast lifted out with care.

Since some bones may weigh as much as two or three hundred pounds, strength is needed as well as carefulness.

Now the cast must be removed and the bones freed from whatever bits of rock may be left on them. If the bones are very large, they may have holes drilled lengthwise through them so that steel rods can be pushed through to help support their weight. Smaller bones are just given more coats of shellac to protect them from the air.

Now you have the bones in good condition. But just a lot of assorted bones are of very little interest to people who come to the museum to get some idea of what dinosaurs were like. To make a good exhibit, the bones must be put together to form a skeleton.

Assembling a dinosaur skeleton is no one-man job. It takes a team of skilled and highly trained scientists and technical assistants. And it takes a long time.

First of all of course they must be certain what kind of creature the bones belonged to. Each bone must be compared with others until it has been identified.

Then a good, lively, life-like pose must be picked. It often takes a good deal of study to figure out just what would have been a typical pose for Anhylosaurus or Struthiomimus, if you have encountered them only as a group of dusty and often disordered bones.

Probably some of the bones are missing too. These must be identified and replaced with plaster. When all the bones are on hand, and assembled in more or less the correct order, a frame is made to hold up the bones as they are raised into place. Irons and chains are used to support the bones after they have been strung together, something like a puppet on strings. At last, when the framework is removed, the skeleton stands firmly in a life-like pose, with its supports so skillfully placed that they can scarcely be seen.

Perhaps if this is a specially fine specimen, the scientists may decide to do a restoration. Working with an artist, they figure out how the dinosaur's muscles were strung on his bones, how his skin fitted over bones and muscles, and what color he might have been. They may even set him in a bit of his own native countryside, beautifully built up, based on the scientist's knowledge of ancient climates and plant life and using all the artist's skill.

Then he is labeled, with his full scientific name and a note as to where he lived and when. And visitors to the museum can get a glimpse into the long-vanished, mysterious world of the wonderful dinosaurs.

The fossil bones are raised to position in a museum hall.

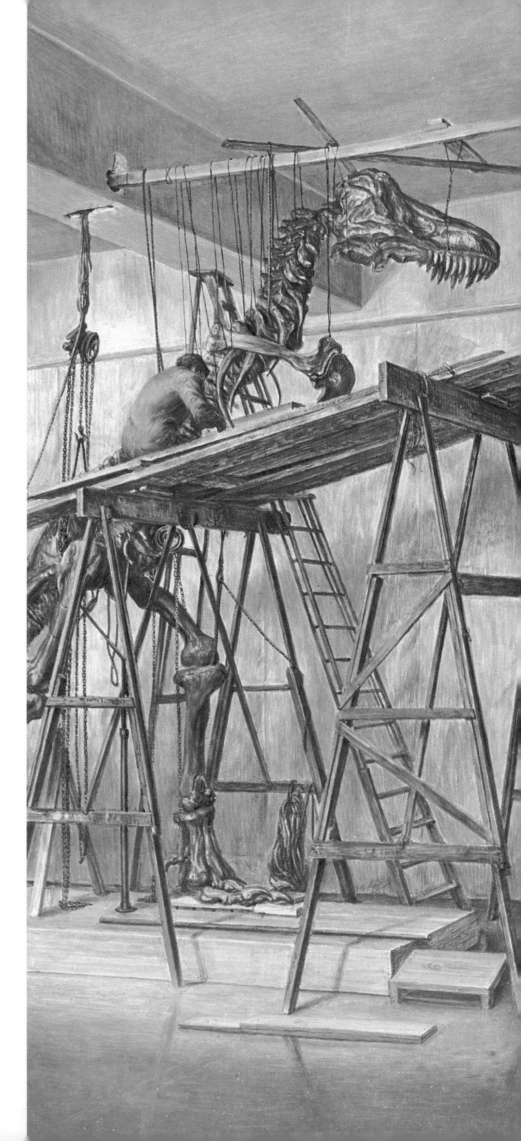

Index and Guide to Pronunciation

Asterisks (*) denote pages on which the subjects are illustrated.

CERATOPSIANS
(horned dinosaurs)

ORNITHOPODS
(duck-billed dinosaurs)

THEROPODS
(carnivorous dinosaurs)

ORNITHOPODS
(duck-billed dinosaurs)

ANKYLOSAURS
(armored dinosaurs)

SAUROPODS
(giant dinosaurs)

THEROPODS
(carnivorous dinosaurs)